Building
a Bridge

Building a Bridge

by Lisa Shook Begaye

illustrated by Libba Tracy

rising moon

Books for Young Readers from Northland Publishing

FIRST EDITION, 1993
ISBN 0-87358-557-7

FIRST SOFTCOVER PRINTING, 1998
ISBN 0-87358-727-8

Library of Congress Cataloging-in-Publication Data

Begaye, Lisa Shook.
Building a bridge / by Lisa Shook Begaye ; illustrated by Libba Tracy. — 1st ed.
p. cm.
Summary: On the first day of kindergarten, with the help of their
teacher, a Navajo girl and an Anglo girl learn to overlook their
different appearances and become friends.
[1. Friendship—Fiction. 2. Race relations—Fiction. 3. Navajo
Indians—Fiction. 4. Indians of North America—Southwest, New—
Fiction. 5. Schools—Fiction.] I. Tracy, Libba, ill. II. Title.
PZ7.B388214Bu 1993
[E]—dc20   92-82138
Designed by Rudy J. Ramos
Cover design and art direction by David Jenney
Printed in Hong Kong by Wing King Tong

.0723/2M/6-98

To the people of the Navajo Nation,
many of whom have gone out of their way
not only to build a bridge
but to walk across it.

—L. S. B.

I dedicate this book to teachers who so unselfishly give of their hearts and spirits to make a difference with young people. My husband, Tom, is such an individual, and I deeply thank him and every other inspired educator for their magnificence and generosity of self.

—L. T.

The first day of school is always a little scary and a little exciting. For Anna, the scary and the exciting were all jumbled up, making her tummy full of butterflies and bouncy rubber balls.

But Anna was a big girl now. Her mommy said so all the time. So she tied her shoes, buttoned her jacket, and got ready to walk to the school bus.

While Anna prepared for school, Juanita, on another part of the Reservation, got ready, too. She had gotten up very early, even before light peeped through the hogan door. She herded the sheep from their pen and helped her mother mix dough for the fry bread. She would carry some fry bread to Grandmother on her way to the school bus.

▲　■　●

Juanita thought the first day of school was a little scary and a little exciting. She had a tummy full of butterflies and bouncy rubber balls, but she was a big girl now. Her mother said so all the time.

Juanita tied her shoes, buttoned her jacket, and after greeting her grandmother and giving her some fry bread, she walked to the school bus.

As Anna waited at the bus stop, she saw the school bus coming down the road from the Reservation. Her mother had explained to Anna that most of the children she would be going to school with were Navajo Indians. Anna had seen a few of the dark-skinned, dark-haired people when she had gone with her daddy to see where he worked. But nothing Anna's mommy said had prepared her for all the boys and girls who were seated in the school bus. They looked just like each other and none of them had blond hair or light skin like hers!

"I don't think I'm going to have any friends here," she thought. "I don't like all these different-looking people."

The boys and girls stared at the little girl with the light hair. She really looked different.

The bus rolled on toward the little school just off the Navajo Reservation.

When the bus stopped, the children headed for their classrooms. Anna and Juanita were in the same kindergarten room. They hung their coats on the hooks in the coat closet and joined the other children on the big rug.

"*Yá'át'ééh (ya-ta-Hey)* and hello, boys and girls!" said Mrs. Yazzie, the kindergarten teacher. The children all greeted Mrs. Yazzie and began their day at school.

When playtime came, Anna sat quietly by herself, watching the other children play. She still felt like she didn't fit in with the other children because she looked so different from them.

Mrs. Yazzie called Juanita to her. "Juanita, would you please take the blocks over to Anna and see if she would like to help you build something?"

Juanita asked Anna if she wanted to play with her. Anna nodded.

"Those blocks are magic," Mrs. Yazzie told the girls.

Juanita and
Anna looked at the
blocks and then
at each other.
They couldn't
understand
how plain old
purple and
green blocks
could be magic,
but they played
with them just
the same.

"Let's share the blocks," Anna said.

"Okay, you take half and I'll take half," said Juanita.

So Anna picked out all the green ones and Juanita took all the purple ones.

"What do you want to build?" Anna asked.

"Let's see who can build a bridge the fastest," Juanita replied.

So Anna and Juanita set about building their bridges.

When they had finished, they discovered
something very interesting. Anna had built a
green bridge exactly like Juanita's purple one.
Mrs. Yazzie smiled at the girls. The magic of
the blocks was working.

"Do you want to know a secret, girls?" Mrs. Yazzie asked. Anna and Juanita smiled and nodded. "If you put all your blocks together and mix them up, you can build a great big bridge. It doesn't matter what color the blocks are, they all fit together."

▲　■　●

Juanita and Anna tore down their own bridges and began building one big purple and green bridge. The bigger the bridge got, the more excited they grew. Soon, they were dancing around and hugging each other. It was fun to work together on the bridge.

As the big yellow school bus rolled
home, Anna and Juanita sat together talking
about all the things they could build with
the green and purple blocks. It was okay
that the blocks were different colors.
Differences make things magical.

While Anna and Juanita sat on the bus deciding that they were best friends, Mrs. Yazzie was turning out the lights in the kindergarten room. As she glanced back she smiled at the very pretty, very important, very magical bridge.

About the Author

LISA SHOOK BEGAYE is an actress and writer whose husband, Rex Begaye, is a full-blooded Navajo and an award-winning professional artist. Because of their careers, they travel approximately eleven months out of the year. In her many stops across the country, Lisa is often asked if it is difficult being married to a Native American. She responds that although each of their cultures is very important and very different, it is possible to join them and have something positive emerge.

About the Illustrator

LIBBA TRACY has been an illustrator for the past thirteen years, working primarily in watercolor. A resident of Phoenix, Arizona, Libba feels that being close to the vibrancy and subtleties of the desert is vital to her work; she is quick to notice the color of shadows or the shape of a cholla in the desert light. Her first children's book, *This House Is Made of Mud* (Northland, 1991), written by Ken Buchanan, was honored with the 1992 Arizona Author Award and was also selected to be featured on the PBS television program "Reading Rainbow."